The Entrepreneurial Mindset

- *Dhairyashil Picharute*

INDEX

Introduction

The Entrepreneurial Mindset is a book that explores the key characteristics, skills, and habits that are essential for success as an entrepreneur. Whether you are starting your own business or working within an established organization, developing an entrepreneurial mindset can help you to achieve your goals and overcome the challenges that you will encounter along the way.

In this book, we will examine the different elements of the entrepreneurial mindset, including developing a growth mindset, overcoming fear and taking risks, resilience and perseverance, creativity and innovation, customer-centric thinking, financial management, marketing and sales, building a strong brand, embracing change and adaptability, creating a culture of innovation, managing time and priorities, and building and managing high-performing teams.

Through real-life examples, practical advice, and actionable tips, this book will help you to cultivate the mindset and skills needed to succeed as an entrepreneur. Whether you are just starting out or are a seasoned entrepreneur, The Entrepreneurial Mindset is a must-read for anyone looking to achieve success in business and in life. So, let's dive in and explore the world of entrepreneurship together!

Chapter 1: Characteristics of the Entrepreneurial Mindset

1. Visionary Thinking:

Entrepreneurs possess the ability to think big and see opportunities where others may not. They are not satisfied with the status quo and are always looking for ways to improve or disrupt existing systems. They have a clear and compelling vision for their business and are able to communicate it effectively to others, inspiring them to support their vision.

To develop visionary thinking, entrepreneurs must cultivate a mindset of creativity and innovation. They must be able to think outside the box and embrace unconventional ideas. They must also be able to develop a clear and compelling vision for their business, as well as a plan to achieve it.

2. Risk-taking:

Entrepreneurs are not afraid to take risks, which is essential for achieving success in business. They understand that failure is a natural part of the entrepreneurial journey and are willing to take calculated risks to achieve their goals. By taking risks, entrepreneurs are able to break through barriers and overcome obstacles that might otherwise hold them back.

To develop risk-taking, entrepreneurs must be comfortable with uncertainty and be willing to take calculated risks. They must be able to assess potential risks and develop strategies to mitigate them. They must also be able to learn from their failures and use them as opportunities to grow and improve.

3. Persistence:

Entrepreneurs are persistent and determined. They are able to maintain their motivation and stay focused on their goals, even in the face of setbacks and challenges. This persistence is what enables entrepreneurs to keep moving forward and ultimately achieve success.

To develop persistence, entrepreneurs must cultivate a growth mindset and be willing to learn from their failures. They must be able to stay motivated and maintain a positive attitude, even when things get tough. They must also be able to adapt their strategies and approaches as needed to overcome obstacles.

4. Creativity:

Entrepreneurs are creative problem-solvers who are able to come up with innovative solutions to complex problems. They are not satisfied with the status quo and are always looking for ways to improve or disrupt existing systems. This creativity is what enables entrepreneurs to differentiate themselves from the competition and create new opportunities.

To develop creativity, entrepreneurs must cultivate a mindset of curiosity and a willingness to explore new ideas. They must be able to challenge conventional thinking and be open to new perspectives.

They must also be able to identify and solve problems in creative ways.

5. Passion:

Entrepreneurs are passionate about what they do. They have a deep sense of purpose and are committed to their business and their customers. This passion is what gives entrepreneurs the drive and motivation they need to succeed.

To develop passion, entrepreneurs must be able to align their values and beliefs with their business goals. They must be able to identify what they are passionate about and use that to drive their work. They must also be able to maintain their motivation and enthusiasm, even in the face of challenges and setbacks.

6. Flexibility:

Entrepreneurs are flexible and adaptable. They are able to adjust to changing circumstances and are not afraid to pivot their business when necessary. This flexibility is what enables entrepreneurs to stay agile and responsive to market conditions.

To develop flexibility, entrepreneurs must be able to embrace change and be open to new ideas and opportunities. They must be able to adapt their strategies and approaches as needed to respond to changing market conditions. They must also be able to stay nimble and responsive to new developments.

7. Resourcefulness:

Entrepreneurs are resourceful and able to make the most of limited resources. They are able to find creative ways to bootstrap their business and to leverage their network of contacts to achieve their goals. This resourcefulness is what enables entrepreneurs to achieve their goals without relying on external funding or resources.

To develop resourcefulness, entrepreneurs must be able to identify and leverage their existing resources Sure, here are a few more points to consider in chapter 1 on the characteristics of the entrepreneurial mindset:

8. Resilience:

Entrepreneurship is a challenging journey, and entrepreneurs must be able to bounce back from setbacks and failures. Resilience is the ability to recover quickly from adversity and keep moving forward. Entrepreneurs must be able to maintain their motivation and determination, even when things get tough.

To develop resilience, entrepreneurs must be able to cultivate a growth mindset and embrace failures as opportunities to learn and grow. They must be able to stay focused on their goals and maintain a positive attitude, even in the face of setbacks. They must also be able to seek support from their network and take care of their physical and mental health.

9. Goal-orientation:

Entrepreneurs are highly goal-oriented and have a clear vision of what they want to achieve. They are able to break down their goals into actionable steps and develop a plan to achieve them. This goal-orientation is what enables entrepreneurs to stay focused and motivated on their journey.

To develop goal-orientation, entrepreneurs must be able to identify their long-term vision and break it down into smaller, achievable goals. They must be able to prioritize their tasks and stay focused on their most important goals. They must also be able to measure their progress and adjust their approach as needed to achieve their goals.

10. Customer Focus:

Entrepreneurs are customer-centric and focused on delivering value to their customers. They are able to identify their customers' needs and develop products and services that meet those needs. This customer focus is what enables entrepreneurs to create loyal customers and build a sustainable business.

To develop customer focus, entrepreneurs must be able to understand their customers' needs and preferences. They must be able to collect feedback and use it to improve their products and services. They must also be able to build relationships with their customers and create a positive customer experience.

11. Action-Oriented:

Entrepreneurs are action-oriented and focused on taking decisive action to achieve their goals. They are able to make decisions quickly and take calculated risks to move their business forward. This action-oriented mindset is what enables entrepreneurs to make progress and achieve their goals.

To develop an action-oriented mindset, entrepreneurs must be able to identify opportunities and take decisive action to pursue them. They must be able to make decisions quickly and take calculated risks. They must also be able to prioritize their tasks and stay focused on their most important goals.

12. Self-discipline:

Entrepreneurs must be self-disciplined and able to stay focused on their goals. They must be able to manage their time effectively and avoid distractions that can hinder their progress. This self-discipline is what enables entrepreneurs to stay productive and make progress on their journey.

To develop self-discipline, entrepreneurs must be able to set clear goals and prioritize their tasks. They must be able to manage their time effectively and avoid distractions. They must also be able to hold themselves accountable for their progress and take responsibility for their actions.

Overall, the entrepreneurial mindset is a unique set of characteristics and traits that enable entrepreneurs to create successful businesses and make a positive impact on the world. Developing these characteristics requires a combination of mindset, skills, and experience, and can be cultivated over time through deliberate practice and a willingness to learn and grow. By understanding the key characteristics of the entrepreneurial mindset, aspiring entrepreneurs can better prepare themselves for the challenges and opportunities of entrepreneurship.

66

"Your level of success will rarely exceed your level of personal development because success is something you attract by the person you become."

HAL ELROD

OBERLO

Chapter 2: The Importance of Opportunity Identification

Entrepreneurship is all about identifying and pursuing opportunities. Opportunity identification is the process of recognizing and assessing potential business opportunities. It is a critical step in the entrepreneurial journey because it determines the direction and focus of the business. In this chapter, we will discuss the importance of opportunity identification and explore the key factors that entrepreneurs should consider when identifying opportunities.

1. Why is Opportunity Identification Important?
Opportunity identification is important for several reasons:

a. Determines the viability of the business idea:
Identifying a good business opportunity is the first step towards building a successful business. By evaluating the potential of an opportunity, entrepreneurs can determine whether the business idea is worth pursuing or not.

b. Helps in setting goals and direction:
Once a good opportunity is identified, entrepreneurs can set goals and direction for their

business. They can create a clear vision and mission for the business and establish a roadmap to achieve their objectives.

c. Provides a competitive advantage:

By identifying unique and innovative opportunities, entrepreneurs can gain a competitive advantage over others in the market. They can create a niche market for their business and differentiate themselves from competitors.

d. Increases the chances of success:

By identifying and pursuing good business opportunities, entrepreneurs can increase the chances of success for their business. They can create a sustainable business model and generate profits for their stakeholders.

2. Key Factors to Consider when Identifying Opportunities

When identifying opportunities, entrepreneurs should consider the following key factors:

a. Market demand:

Entrepreneurs should evaluate the market demand for their product or service. They should identify whether there is a need for their offering in the market and whether customers are willing to pay for it.

b. Industry trends:

Entrepreneurs should analyze industry trends and assess whether their business idea aligns with the current trends. They should identify emerging trends and potential changes in the market that could affect their business.

c. Competition:

Entrepreneurs should evaluate the competition in the market. They should identify their competitors and assess their strengths and weaknesses. They should also identify gaps in the market that their competitors are not addressing.

d. Resources:

Entrepreneurs should evaluate the resources required to pursue the opportunity. They should identify the financial, human, and technological resources needed to build the business. They should also assess their own strengths and weaknesses and identify any skill gaps that need to be filled.

e. Legal and regulatory environment:

Entrepreneurs should be aware of the legal and regulatory environment of the industry. They should identify any legal or regulatory hurdles that could hinder their business and develop a plan to mitigate them.

3. Tools and Techniques for Opportunity Identification

Entrepreneurs can use several tools and techniques to identify potential business opportunities:

a. SWOT analysis:

A SWOT analysis is a framework for evaluating the strengths, weaknesses, opportunities, and threats of a business idea. It can help entrepreneurs identify the potential of their business idea and develop a plan to address any weaknesses or threats.

b. Market research:

Market research involves collecting and analyzing data on the market and customers. It can help entrepreneurs identify the market demand for their product or service, assess the competition, and identify emerging trends.

c. Networking:

Networking involves building relationships with other entrepreneurs, industry experts, and potential customers. It can help entrepreneurs identify potential business opportunities, gain insights into the industry, and develop a network of contacts that can help them in their business.

d. Brainstorming:

Brainstorming is a technique for generating creative ideas. It involves generating as many ideas as possible, without judging or evaluating them. Entrepreneurs can use brainstorming to identify potential business opportunities and generate new ideas for their business.

4. Challenges of Opportunity Identification

Opportunity identification is not an easy task and it comes with its own set of challenges. Some of the common challenges that entrepreneurs face while identifying opportunities include.

a. Lack of knowledge and experience:

Entrepreneurs who are new to the industry may lack the knowledge and experience to identify potential business opportunities. They may not be aware of the latest trends, technologies, or customer preferences that could affect their business.

b. Confirmation bias:

Confirmation bias is the tendency to search for information that confirms one's pre-existing beliefs or assumptions. Entrepreneurs may have a confirmation bias towards their own ideas and may not be open to exploring new opportunities that don't align with their beliefs.

c. Overestimating the market demand: Entrepreneurs may overestimate the market demand for their product or service. They may assume that there is a need for their offering in the market without conducting proper market research.

d. Underestimating the competition:

Entrepreneurs may underestimate the competition in the market. They may assume that there are no competitors or that their competitors are not a threat to their business.

e. Limited resources:

Entrepreneurs may have limited resources to pursue the opportunity. They may not have the financial, human, or technological resources to build the business.

5. Tips for Effective Opportunity Identification

To overcome these challenges and identify good business opportunities, entrepreneurs can follow these tips:

a. Keep an open mind:

Entrepreneurs should keep an open mind and be willing to explore new ideas and opportunities. They should be open to feedback and suggestions from others.

b. Conduct proper market research:

Entrepreneurs should conduct proper market research to assess the market demand for their product or service, identify the competition, and analyze industry trends.

c. Network with industry experts:

Entrepreneurs should network with industry experts, potential customers, and other entrepreneurs. They can gain insights into the industry, identify potential opportunities, and develop a network of contacts that can help them in their business.

d. Embrace failure:

Entrepreneurs should embrace failure as a learning opportunity. They should not be afraid to try new ideas and take risks. They should learn from their failures and use those lessons to improve their business.

e. Build a diverse team:

Entrepreneurs should build a diverse team with a range of skills and experiences. This can help them identify new opportunities and address any skill gaps that may exist in the team.

In conclusion, opportunity identification is a critical step in the entrepreneurial journey. It is the first step towards building a successful business. By identifying and pursuing good business opportunities, entrepreneurs can create a sustainable business model, gain a competitive advantage, and generate profits for their stakeholders. However, identifying good business opportunities is not an easy task and it comes with its own set of challenges. Entrepreneurs should keep an open mind, conduct proper market research, network with industry experts, embrace failure, and build a diverse team to overcome these challenges and identify good business opportunities.

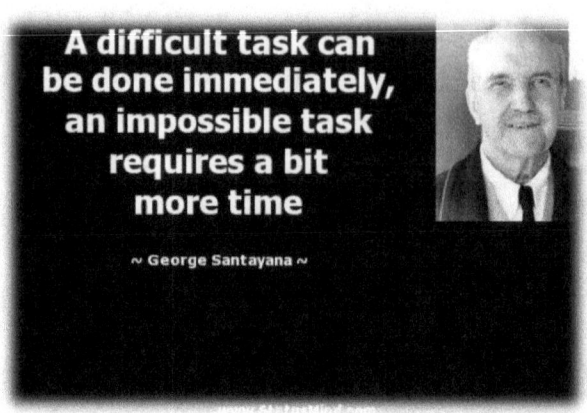

A difficult task can be done immediately, an impossible task requires a bit more time

~ George Santayana ~

Chapter 3: The Role of Risk-Taking

1. Introduction: -

Risk-taking is an integral part of the entrepreneurial mindset. Entrepreneurs are willing to take calculated risks to achieve their goals and build successful businesses. In this chapter, we will discuss the role of risk-taking in entrepreneurship, the benefits of taking risks, and the strategies that entrepreneurs can use to manage risks effectively.

2. The Role of Risk-Taking in Entrepreneurship

Risk-taking is essential for entrepreneurship because it enables entrepreneurs to pursue opportunities that have the potential for significant rewards. Without taking risks, entrepreneurs may miss out on opportunities that could help them grow their business and achieve their goals. Taking risks involves making decisions based on incomplete information and uncertain outcomes. Entrepreneurs who are willing to take risks are more likely to succeed because they are willing to try new things and experiment with different approaches.

3. Benefits of Taking Risks

a. Innovation:

Taking risks can lead to innovation. By trying new things and experimenting with different approaches, entrepreneurs can develop new products, services, and business models that can set them apart from their competitors.

b. Competitive Advantage:

Taking risks can help entrepreneurs gain a competitive advantage. By being the first to market with a new product or service, entrepreneurs can establish themselves as industry leaders and gain a significant market share.

c. Learning Opportunities:

Taking risks provides entrepreneurs with learning opportunities. Even if their risk does not pay off, entrepreneurs can learn valuable lessons that can help them improve their business and make better decisions in the future.

d. Increased Confidence:

Taking risks can increase an entrepreneur's confidence. By successfully taking risks and achieving their goals, entrepreneurs can gain the confidence to take on bigger challenges and pursue even greater opportunities.

4. Strategies for Managing Risks

a. Conduct Proper Risk Analysis:

Entrepreneurs should conduct a proper risk analysis before making any decisions. They should evaluate the potential risks and rewards associated with a particular opportunity and assess whether they have the resources and capabilities to manage those risks.

b. Develop a Risk Management Plan:

Entrepreneurs should develop a risk management plan that outlines how they will manage the risks associated with their business. This plan should include contingency plans for potential risks and strategies for mitigating those risks.

c. Diversify Risk:

Entrepreneurs should diversify their risk by spreading their investments across multiple opportunities. This can help them reduce the impact of any one particular risk and ensure that they have multiple sources of revenue.

d. Stay Informed:

Entrepreneurs should stay informed about industry trends, market conditions, and potential risks. By staying informed, entrepreneurs can identify potential risks and take steps to mitigate them before they become major issues.

5. Types of Risks in Entrepreneurship
There are several types of risks that entrepreneurs face in their business endeavours. These include financial risk, market risk, operational risk, strategic risk, and reputational risk.

a. Financial Risk:
Financial risk refers to the risk of loss due to factors such as changes in interest rates, exchange rates, and credit risk. Entrepreneurs must be careful when making financial decisions and ensure that they have adequate financial resources to manage any potential risks.

b. Market Risk:
Market risk refers to the risk of loss due to changes in market conditions, including shifts in consumer preferences, changes in technology, and shifts in industry trends. Entrepreneurs must stay up-to-date with market trends and anticipate changes to avoid being caught off guard by sudden market shifts.

c. Operational Risk:
Operational risk refers to the risk of loss due to factors such as equipment failure, human error, and natural disasters. Entrepreneurs must have proper

systems in place to manage these risks and ensure that they can quickly respond to any operational disruptions.

d. Strategic Risk:

Strategic risk refers to the risk of loss due to factors such as changes in competition, changes in regulations, and shifts in industry dynamics. Entrepreneurs must be strategic in their decision-making and anticipate potential risks to their business model.

e. Reputational Risk:

Reputational risk refers to the risk of loss due to damage to the entrepreneur's brand and reputation. Entrepreneurs must maintain high ethical standards and ensure that their business practices align with their values to avoid any damage to their reputation.

6. Benefits of Effective Risk Management

Effective risk management can help entrepreneurs minimize the impact of potential risks and ensure that they are well-prepared to manage any challenges that may arise. By managing risks effectively, entrepreneurs can:

a. Protect their Business:

Effective risk management can help entrepreneurs protect their business from potential threats, including financial losses, reputational damage, and operational disruptions.

b. Improve Decision-Making:

Effective risk management can help entrepreneurs make better decisions by providing them with a clear understanding of the potential risks and rewards associated with a particular opportunity.

c. Enhance Long-Term Growth:

Effective risk management can help entrepreneurs enhance their long-term growth prospects by enabling them to take advantage of opportunities that align with their risk tolerance and business objectives.

d. Increase Stakeholder Confidence:

Effective risk management can increase stakeholder confidence in the entrepreneur's ability to manage their business effectively and achieve their goals.

In conclusion, risk-taking is an essential component of the entrepreneurial mindset. Entrepreneurs who are willing to take risks can reap significant rewards, including innovation, competitive advantage, learning opportunities, and increased confidence. However, risk-taking also involves managing risks effectively. Entrepreneurs must be able to identify potential risks, assess their potential impact, and develop strategies to manage those risks effectively. By managing risks effectively, entrepreneurs can protect their business, improve decision-making, enhance long-

term growth prospects, and increase stakeholder confidence.

If you risk nothing, then you risk everything.
- Geena Davis

EVERYDAY**POWER**

Chapter 4: Adaptability and Flexibility

Adaptability and flexibility are critical components of the entrepreneurial mindset. Entrepreneurs face a constantly evolving business landscape, and the ability to adapt quickly and be flexible in their approach can be the difference between success and failure. In this chapter, we will explore the importance of adaptability and flexibility in entrepreneurship and discuss how entrepreneurs can cultivate these traits.

1. What is Adaptability?

Adaptability refers to the ability to adjust to changing circumstances and environments quickly. It involves being open to new ideas, being able to learn from experience, and being able to embrace change. In entrepreneurship, adaptability is essential because entrepreneurs face a rapidly changing business environment, with new technologies, market trends, and consumer preferences emerging all the time.

2. The Importance of Adaptability in Entrepreneurship

Entrepreneurs who are adaptable have several advantages, including:

a. Innovation:

Entrepreneurs who are adaptable can quickly respond to changes in the market and develop innovative solutions to address emerging challenges and opportunities.

b. Competitive Advantage:

Entrepreneurs who are adaptable can quickly pivot their business model to stay ahead of the competition and take advantage of new opportunities.

c. Learning Opportunities:

Entrepreneurs who are adaptable are open to learning and can quickly adapt their strategies based on new information and feedback.

d. Resilience:

Entrepreneurs who are adaptable can quickly recover from setbacks and adapt their approach to overcome obstacles.

3. What is Flexibility?

Flexibility refers to the ability to change course quickly and make adjustments to plans as needed. In entrepreneurship, flexibility is essential because plans often change, and entrepreneurs must be able to adjust their approach to stay on track.

4. The Importance of Flexibility in Entrepreneurship

Entrepreneurs who are flexible have several advantages, including:

a. Agility:

Entrepreneurs who are flexible can quickly adjust their plans to respond to changes in the market or unexpected obstacles.

b. Resourcefulness:

Entrepreneurs who are flexible can find creative solutions to problems and make the most of limited resources.

c. Customer Focus:

Entrepreneurs who are flexible can quickly adapt their products or services to meet the changing needs and preferences of their customers.

d. Collaboration:

Entrepreneurs who are flexible are more open to collaboration and partnership, which can help them access new resources and opportunities.

5. Cultivating Adaptability and Flexibility

Adaptability and flexibility are traits that can be developed and strengthened over time. Here are some tips for entrepreneurs looking to cultivate these traits:

a. Embrace Change: Entrepreneurs must learn to embrace change and be open to new ideas and approaches.

b. Stay Agile: Entrepreneurs must be able to quickly adjust their plans and strategies to respond to changes in the market or unexpected obstacles.

c. Learn from Experience: Entrepreneurs must be willing to learn from their experiences and be open to feedback from customers and stakeholders.

d. Build Resilience: Entrepreneurs must build resilience and be able to bounce back from setbacks and failures.

e. Stay Customer-Focused: Entrepreneurs must stay focused on the needs and preferences of their customers and be willing to adapt their products or services to meet those needs.

6. The Relationship Between Adaptability, Flexibility, and Innovation

Innovation is at the heart of entrepreneurship, and it requires both adaptability and flexibility. Entrepreneurs must be adaptable to identify new opportunities and adjust their approach as they gain new insights into the market and their customers' needs. Flexibility is essential in allowing entrepreneurs to change course quickly when needed and take advantage of emerging trends and opportunities.

7. The Importance of Creativity in Entrepreneurship

Creativity is a crucial component of entrepreneurship and involves generating new and innovative ideas and solutions to problems. Entrepreneurs who are creative can develop products or services that meet the changing needs and preferences of their customers, and they can differentiate themselves from the competition by offering unique solutions to problems.

8. Cultivating Creativity

Entrepreneurs can cultivate creativity by:

a. Encouraging Divergent Thinking:

Entrepreneurs can encourage divergent thinking by creating an environment that fosters creativity and allows for the exploration of new ideas.

b. Embracing Risk:

Entrepreneurs must be willing to take risks and try new things, even if they may not always be successful.

c. Embracing Failure:

Entrepreneurs must embrace failure as an opportunity to learn and grow, rather than as a setback.

d. Collaborating with Others:
Collaborating with others can lead to new and innovative ideas, as well as the sharing of resources and knowledge.

e. Continuously Learning:
Entrepreneurs must continuously learn and seek out new information and perspectives to expand their knowledge and generate new ideas.

9. Overcoming Barriers to Creativity
Entrepreneurs may face several barriers to creativity, such as fear of failure, lack of resources, and a rigid mindset. However, by adopting an adaptive and flexible approach, entrepreneurs can overcome these barriers and cultivate creativity.

Conclusion
Innovation and creativity are critical components of entrepreneurship, and both require adaptability and flexibility. Entrepreneurs who are adaptable and flexible can quickly adjust their approach to take advantage of emerging trends and opportunities, while those who are creative can develop unique and innovative solutions to problems. By cultivating these traits and adopting an adaptive and flexible approach, entrepreneurs can increase their chances of success in a rapidly changing business environment.

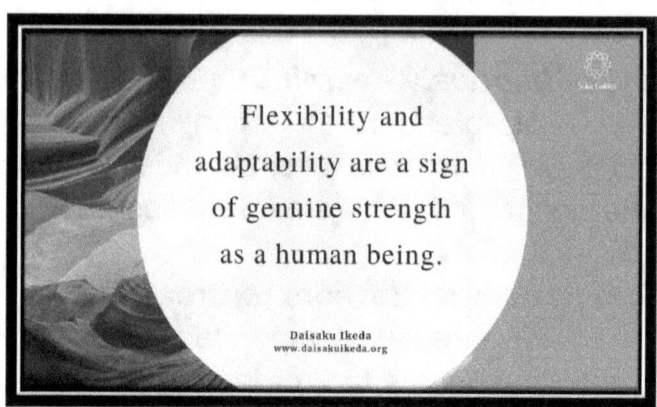

Flexibility and
adaptability are a sign
of genuine strength
as a human being.

Daisaku Ikeda
www.daisakuikeda.org

Chapter 5: Resilience and Perseverance

Resilience and perseverance are crucial characteristics of the entrepreneurial mindset. In Chapter 4, we discussed the importance of adaptability and flexibility, which enable entrepreneurs to adjust to changes and overcome challenges. In this chapter, we will delve deeper into the role of resilience and perseverance in entrepreneurship.

1. Resilience

Resilience refers to the ability to bounce back from setbacks, challenges, and adversity. In the context of entrepreneurship, resilience means being able to handle failure, rejection, and other obstacles without losing motivation or giving up. Resilient entrepreneurs are able to keep moving forward and remain focused on their goals despite setbacks and challenges.

2. Perseverance

Perseverance refers to the ability to persist in the face of obstacles and challenges. It involves having the determination and tenacity to keep working towards a goal, even when progress is slow or setbacks occur. Persevering entrepreneurs are able to maintain their focus and keep pushing towards their objectives, even when faced with significant challenges.

3. The Importance of Resilience and Perseverance in Entrepreneurship

Entrepreneurship is a challenging and unpredictable journey, and resilience and perseverance are essential traits for success. In the face of setbacks, challenges, and uncertainty, entrepreneurs must be able to stay focused on their goals and keep pushing forward. Resilience and perseverance enable entrepreneurs to weather the ups and downs of the entrepreneurial journey and emerge stronger on the other side.

4. Building Resilience and Perseverance

Entrepreneurs can cultivate resilience and perseverance by:

a. Developing a Growth Mindset:

Adopting a growth mindset, where failures and setbacks are viewed as opportunities for learning and growth, can help entrepreneurs develop resilience and perseverance.

b. Practicing Self-Care:
Taking care of oneself, both physically and mentally, can help entrepreneurs maintain their energy and motivation in the face of challenges.

c. Seeking Support:
Building a strong support system of mentors, peers, and advisors can provide entrepreneurs with the encouragement and guidance they need to keep moving forward.

d. Setting Realistic Goals:
Setting realistic goals and breaking them down into smaller, achievable steps can help entrepreneurs maintain their motivation and focus.

e. Embracing Failure:
Entrepreneurs must embrace failure as a necessary part of the learning process and be willing to take calculated risks.

5. Overcoming Barriers to Resilience and Perseverance
Entrepreneurs may face several barriers to developing resilience and perseverance, such as fear of failure, lack of support, and burnout. However, by adopting strategies to cultivate these traits,

entrepreneurs can overcome these barriers and build the resilience and perseverance needed for success.

6. Case Study:

Resilience and Perseverance in the Face of Adversity

The story of Sara Blakely, the founder of Spanx, is a great example of resilience and perseverance in entrepreneurship. Blakely had the idea for Spanx while getting ready for a party and realizing she didn't have the right undergarment to wear under a pair of white pants. She cut the feet off a pair of control-top pantyhose and Spanx was born.

Blakely faced multiple setbacks and challenges as she built Spanx from the ground up. She struggled to get a prototype made and had to overcome numerous rejections from potential investors. When she finally got her first big break with a major retailer, she had to figure out how to produce a large volume of products quickly.

Despite these challenges, Blakely persisted. She kept refining her product and pitching to investors until she finally secured funding. She worked tirelessly to grow Spanx, attending trade shows and building relationships with retailers. She even drove around to stores herself, pitching her product and training salespeople on how to sell Spanx.

Blakely's resilience and perseverance paid off. Spanx became a massive success, with sales of over $1 billion and Blakely becoming one of the youngest self-made female billionaires in history.

Conclusion

Resilience and perseverance are essential characteristics of the entrepreneurial mindset, enabling entrepreneurs to overcome setbacks, handle challenges, and persist in the face of adversity. By adopting strategies to cultivate these traits and overcoming barriers to resilience and perseverance, entrepreneurs can increase their chances of success in the competitive and unpredictable world of entrepreneurship. The story of Sara Blakely and Spanx is just one example of how these traits can lead to great success.

Chapter 6: Building a Strong Network

Building a strong network is essential for any entrepreneur who wants to succeed in their business ventures. Having a strong network can provide entrepreneurs with access to resources, information, and opportunities that can help them grow their businesses, make valuable connections, and establish their brand in the marketplace. In this chapter, we will explore the key strategies that entrepreneurs can use to build a strong network.

The first step to building a strong network is to identify your target audience. Entrepreneurs should have a clear understanding of who their target customers, investors, partners, and mentors are, and then develop a strategy for reaching out to them. This may involve attending networking events, joining industry associations, or reaching out to contacts through social media or email.

Once entrepreneurs have identified their target audience, they should focus on building relationships with them. This means taking the time to get to know people, asking questions, listening to their needs, and offering value in return. Entrepreneurs should also be proactive in reaching out to their contacts and maintaining regular communication with them. This can be achieved through email newsletters, social media updates, or even a phone call or coffee meeting.

In addition to building relationships with individuals, entrepreneurs should also focus on building relationships with organizations and communities. This means becoming involved in industry associations, attending conferences and trade shows, and participating in online forums and discussion groups. By becoming active in these communities, entrepreneurs can gain valuable insights into industry trends, connect with like-minded individuals, and establish themselves as thought leaders in their field.

Another key strategy for building a strong network is to seek out mentors and advisors. These are experienced individuals who can provide entrepreneurs with guidance, advice, and support as they navigate the challenges of entrepreneurship. Mentors and advisors can also provide entrepreneurs with access to their own networks, which can open up new opportunities and connections.

Finally, entrepreneurs should always be looking for ways to give back to their network. This means being generous with their time, knowledge, and resources, and finding ways to help others achieve their goals. By giving back to their network, entrepreneurs can build trust and loyalty, and establish themselves as valuable members of their community.

In addition to the strategies outlined in the previous section, there are several other tactics that entrepreneurs can use to build a strong network:

1. Attend industry events:

Attending conferences, trade shows, and other industry events is a great way to connect with like-minded individuals and build relationships. These events often provide opportunities to meet new people, learn about industry trends, and participate in panel discussions and other activities.

2. Participate in online communities:

There are many online communities and forums where entrepreneurs can connect with others in their industry. By participating in these communities, entrepreneurs can share ideas, ask questions, and establish themselves as thought leaders in their field.

3. Offer value to others:

When building a network, it's important to offer value to others. This can be achieved by sharing knowledge, making introductions, or providing resources and support. By offering value, entrepreneurs can establish themselves as helpful and trustworthy members of their community.

4. Utilize social media:

Social media platforms like LinkedIn, Twitter, and Instagram can be powerful tools for building a network. By sharing updates, engaging with others, and participating in conversations, entrepreneurs can connect with others and expand their reach.

5. Volunteer and get involved in the community:

Volunteering for local organizations or getting involved in community initiatives can provide opportunities to meet new people and build relationships. These activities also allow entrepreneurs to give back to their community and establish themselves as valuable members of the community.

6. Focus on quality over quantity:

When building a network, it's important to focus on quality over quantity. Rather than trying to connect with as many people as possible, entrepreneurs should focus on building meaningful relationships with a select group of individuals who can provide value and support.

In conclusion, building a strong network is a critical component of the entrepreneurial mindset. By utilizing strategies such as attending industry events, participating in online communities, offering value to others, utilizing social media, getting involved in the community, and focusing on quality over quantity, entrepreneurs can build a strong network that can provide support, opportunities, and resources as they grow their business.

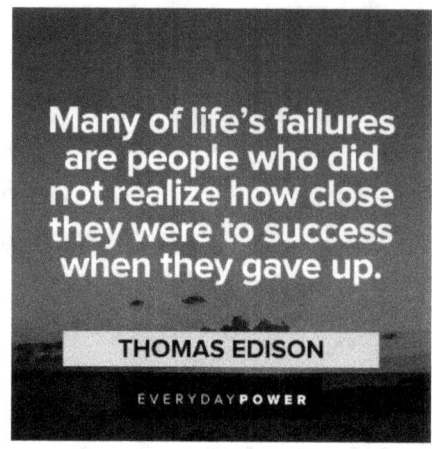

Chapter 7: Overcoming Common Entrepreneurial Challenges

Entrepreneurship is not without its challenges. In this chapter, we will explore some of the common challenges that entrepreneurs face and provide strategies for overcoming them. By understanding these challenges and developing effective coping mechanisms, entrepreneurs can navigate the ups and downs of their entrepreneurial journey more successfully.

1. Managing Uncertainty:

Managing uncertainty is a crucial skill for entrepreneurs. To overcome this challenge, entrepreneurs can:

- Conduct Thorough Market Research:

Understanding the market, industry trends, and customer needs is essential for making informed decisions and mitigating risks. Thorough market research helps entrepreneurs identify potential challenges and opportunities, allowing them to adjust their strategies accordingly.

- Create Contingency Plans:

Developing contingency plans helps entrepreneurs prepare for unforeseen circumstances. By considering various scenarios and creating alternative plans, entrepreneurs can better navigate unexpected challenges and make timely adjustments to their business strategies.

- Stay Adaptable:

Flexibility and adaptability are key traits for entrepreneurs. Being open to change and willing to pivot, when necessary, enables entrepreneurs to respond quickly to market dynamics and seize new opportunities.

- Seek Advice from Mentors or Industry Experts:

Seeking guidance from experienced mentors or industry experts can provide valuable insights and help entrepreneurs gain different perspectives. Mentors can share their own experiences and offer advice on managing uncertainty based on their past successes and failures.

2. Financial Management:

Effective financial management is vital for the long-term success of any business. To overcome financial challenges, entrepreneurs can:

- Develop a Solid Financial Plan:

A well-crafted financial plan outlines projected revenues, expenses, and cash flow. It helps entrepreneurs track their financial performance, make informed decisions, and allocate resources effectively.

- Monitor Expenses:

Keeping a close eye on expenses is crucial, especially during the early stages of a business when resources may be limited. Entrepreneurs should establish a system to track and control expenses, identifying areas where costs can be optimized without compromising quality.

- Explore Various Funding Options:

Entrepreneurs should consider different funding sources, such as bootstrapping, loans, grants, or seeking investments from venture capitalists or angel investors. Exploring a diverse range of funding options allows entrepreneurs to secure the necessary capital to fuel their growth.

- Seek Professional Advice:

Working with accountants or financial advisors can provide entrepreneurs with expert guidance on financial management, tax planning, and compliance. These professionals can help entrepreneurs make informed financial decisions and ensure legal and regulatory compliance.

3. Time Management:

Effective time management is essential for entrepreneurs to maximize productivity and achieve their goals. To overcome time management challenges, entrepreneurs can:

- *Set Clear Goals:*

Defining clear and specific goals helps entrepreneurs prioritize tasks and allocate time accordingly. Setting measurable objectives enables entrepreneurs to track progress and make adjustments as needed.

- *Prioritize Tasks:*

Identifying high-priority tasks and focusing on those that contribute most significantly to business growth and success is crucial. Entrepreneurs should determine which activities require their immediate attention and delegate or outsource non-critical tasks when possible.

- *Delegate Responsibilities:*

Entrepreneurs should leverage their team's skills and capabilities by delegating tasks to capable individuals. Effective delegation not only frees up time for entrepreneurs but also empowers employees and promotes their professional growth.

- Utilize Time Management Tools or Techniques:

There are numerous time management tools and techniques available to entrepreneurs. These tools include project management software, task management apps, and time-tracking tools. Techniques such as the Pomodoro Technique (working in focused bursts with short breaks) can also enhance productivity.

4. Building a Strong Team:

Building a strong team is crucial for entrepreneurial success. To overcome team-building challenges, entrepreneurs can:

- Define Clear Job Roles:

Clearly defining job roles and responsibilities within the organization helps employees understand their expectations and contributes to efficient teamwork. This clarity minimizes confusion and enhances overall productivity.

- Implement Effective Hiring Processes:

Recruiting the right talent is critical for building a strong team. Entrepreneurs should establish effective hiring processes, including creating job descriptions, conducting thorough interviews, and assessing candidates' skills and cultural fit.

- Invest in Employee Development:

Supporting employees' professional growth and development not only enhances their skills but also boosts morale and loyalty

5. Market Competition:
Competition is a constant challenge for entrepreneurs, but there are strategies to overcome it:

- Identify Unique Value Proposition:
Entrepreneurs must clearly define their unique value proposition that sets them apart from competitors. Understanding what makes their products or services distinct and communicating that to their target audience is essential for standing out in a competitive market.

- Continuous Innovation:
To stay ahead of the competition, entrepreneurs must foster a culture of innovation. This involves encouraging employees to think creatively, soliciting customer feedback, and regularly updating products or services to meet evolving customer needs.

- Stay Updated on Industry Trends:
Keeping a pulse on industry trends and market dynamics is crucial for making informed business decisions. Entrepreneurs should stay informed through market research, industry publications, attending conferences, and networking with industry peers.

- Collaborate and Partner:

Collaboration with other businesses or strategic partnerships can be a powerful strategy to overcome competition. By joining forces, entrepreneurs can leverage each other's strengths, access new markets, and create mutually beneficial opportunities.

6. Self-Doubt and Resilience:

Entrepreneurs often face self-doubt and encounter setbacks along their entrepreneurial journey. Building resilience is key to overcoming these challenges:

- Maintain a Positive Mindset:

Developing a positive mindset helps entrepreneurs stay motivated and focused. They should cultivate optimism, embrace failure as a learning opportunity, and celebrate small wins to build momentum.

- Seek Support from Mentors or Support Networks:

Having a strong support system is crucial. Entrepreneurs can benefit from connecting with mentors, joining entrepreneurial communities, or seeking guidance from peer groups. These support networks provide encouragement, advice, and valuable insights.

- Learn from Failures:

Instead of letting failures discourage them, entrepreneurs should embrace them as valuable learning experiences. Analyzing failures, identifying lessons, and applying those lessons to future endeavors can help entrepreneurs bounce back stronger.

- Practice Self-Care:

Entrepreneurs must prioritize self-care to maintain physical and mental well-being. This includes getting enough rest, exercising regularly, practicing mindfulness or meditation, and engaging in activities that recharge and rejuvenate them.

7. Scaling and Growth:

Scaling a business presents its own unique set of challenges. Entrepreneurs can overcome these challenges through strategic planning and execution:

- Develop Scalable Processes:

Entrepreneurs should focus on developing systems and processes that can accommodate growth. This involves automating tasks, streamlining operations, and ensuring scalability in areas such as production, customer service, and supply chain management.

- Leverage Technology:

Technology plays a crucial role in scaling a business efficiently. Entrepreneurs should leverage digital tools and platforms to automate processes, analyze data, improve efficiency, and enhance customer experiences.

- Hire Strategically:

Scaling requires assembling a competent team. Entrepreneurs should carefully assess their hiring needs, identify talent gaps, and recruit individuals with the right skills and cultural fit to support the company's growth trajectory.

- Focus on Customer Satisfaction:

Maintaining a strong focus on customer satisfaction is vital during scaling. Entrepreneurs should invest in customer support systems, gather feedback, and adapt their offerings to meet evolving customer needs, ensuring a positive customer experience even as the business grows.

8. Balancing Work and Personal Life:

Entrepreneurs often struggle with finding a balance between work and personal life. Here are some strategies to achieve a healthy work-life balance:

- Establish Boundaries:

Setting clear boundaries between work and personal life is essential. Entrepreneurs should define specific working hours, allocate time for personal activities, and communicate these boundaries to their team and stakeholders.

- Prioritize Self-Care:

Entrepreneurs must prioritize self-care activities that promote physical and mental well-being. This includes taking breaks, engaging in hobbies, spending quality time with

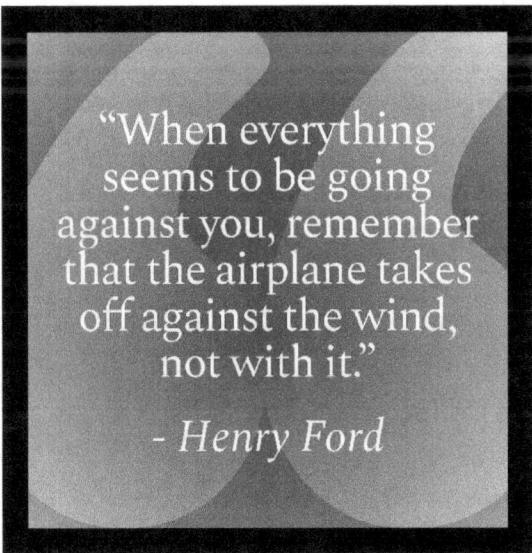

"When everything seems to be going against you, remember that the airplane takes off against the wind, not with it."

- Henry Ford

Chapter 8: The Importance of Continuous Learning

In the fast-paced and ever-changing world of entrepreneurship, continuous learning is crucial for success. This chapter explores the significance of continuous learning for entrepreneurs and provides insights on how to cultivate a mindset of lifelong learning.

1. Embracing Change and Adaptation:

Continuous learning allows entrepreneurs to stay abreast of industry trends, technological advancements, and changing market dynamics. By embracing change and adapting their strategies, entrepreneurs can proactively respond to new opportunities and challenges.

- Stay Informed:

Entrepreneurs should invest time in reading industry publications, attending conferences, and participating in relevant webinars and workshops. This helps them stay up to date with the latest developments in their field.

- Seek Industry Insights:

Engaging with industry experts, joining professional associations, and participating in networking events provide opportunities to gain insights and learn from the experiences of others. Building connections and relationships with fellow entrepreneurs can foster collaborative learning.

- Embrace New Technologies:

Technology is constantly evolving, and entrepreneurs must stay abreast of the latest tools and platforms relevant to their business. Continuous learning allows entrepreneurs to harness the power of technology to improve operations, enhance productivity, and better serve customers.

2. Enhancing Skills and Knowledge:

Continuous learning helps entrepreneurs enhance their skills and expand their knowledge base, enabling them to become more effective in various aspects of their business.

- Develop Business Acumen:

Entrepreneurs can pursue formal education programs or specialized courses to strengthen their understanding of finance, marketing, operations, and other key areas. This enhances their ability to make informed decisions and navigate complex business challenges.

- Acquire Leadership Skills:

Effective leadership is essential for guiding a team and driving business growth. Entrepreneurs can attend leadership training programs, seek mentorship from experienced leaders, or engage in self-study to develop leadership skills.

- Cultivate Creativity:

Continuous learning fosters creativity by exposing entrepreneurs to new ideas, perspectives, and approaches. Engaging in activities such as reading, attending art or design workshops, or exploring diverse fields nurtures creative thinking, which is crucial for innovation and problem-solving.

3. Fostering Adaptability and Resilience:

Entrepreneurship is inherently unpredictable, and continuous learning helps entrepreneurs develop adaptability and resilience to navigate uncertainties and challenges.

- Learn from Failures:

Every failure offers valuable lessons. Entrepreneurs should reflect on their failures, identify areas for improvement, and apply those learnings to future endeavors. This resilience-building mindset transforms failures into opportunities for growth.

- Seek Feedback:

Actively seeking feedback from customers, employees, and mentors provides valuable insights for improvement. Entrepreneurs should embrace constructive criticism and use it to refine their strategies and offerings.

- Embrace New Perspectives:

Continuous learning exposes entrepreneurs to diverse perspectives and ideas. Engaging with individuals from different backgrounds, cultures, and industries broadens their thinking and enhances problem-solving abilities.

4. Stay Competitive and Innovative:

Continuous learning keeps entrepreneurs competitive in the market and fuels innovation, enabling them to differentiate their products or services.

- Monitor Competitors:

Continuous learning includes keeping a watchful eye on competitors. Understanding their strategies, offerings, and customer experiences helps entrepreneurs identify gaps and opportunities for improvement within their own business.

- Foster a Culture of Innovation:

Entrepreneurs can promote a culture of innovation within their organization by encouraging employees to share ideas, experiment, and embrace a growth mindset. Creating platforms for brainstorming and collaboration fosters a culture that values innovation and continuous improvement.

- Experiment and Iterate:

Continuous learning encourages entrepreneurs to experiment with new approaches, products, or services. By adopting an iterative process, entrepreneurs can gather feedback, analyze results, and make necessary adjustments to optimize their offerings.

5. Expanding Professional Network:

Continuous learning provides opportunities to expand one's professional network, fostering collaborations, partnerships, and mentorship.

- Attend Industry Events:

Participating in industry conferences, seminars, and networking events enables entrepreneurs to connect with like-minded individuals and build valuable relationships. These connections can lead to potential business collaborations, partnerships, or even mentorship opportunities.

- Join Online Communities:
Engaging in online communities, forums, and social media groups related to entrepreneurship allows entrepreneurs to connect with a diverse range of individuals. Sharing knowledge, exchanging ideas, and seeking advice within these communities can facilitate continuous learning and professional growth.

- Seek Mentorship:
Mentors play a crucial role in an entrepreneur's journey. Continuously learning from experienced mentors helps entrepreneurs gain insights, avoid common pitfalls, and benefit from their guidance and support.

6. Embracing New Perspectives:
Continuous learning encourages entrepreneurs to explore new perspectives, enabling them to challenge assumptions and think creatively.

- Read Widely:
Reading books, articles, and blogs from a variety of genres broadens an entrepreneur's perspective. By exposing themselves to different viewpoints,

entrepreneurs can gain fresh insights and approaches to problem-solving.

- Engage in Cross-Disciplinary Learning:
Learning from fields outside their own domain expands an entrepreneur's knowledge base and encourages interdisciplinary thinking. Drawing inspiration from diverse disciplines can lead to innovative solutions and unique approaches to business challenges.

- Embrace Cultural Intelligence:
In a globalized world, cultural intelligence is crucial for entrepreneurial success. Continuous learning about different cultures, customs, and communication styles fosters effective cross-cultural collaborations and enhances opportunities in international markets.

7. Enhancing Decision-Making Skills:
Continuous learning equips entrepreneurs with the knowledge and tools to make informed decisions.

- Analyze Case Studies:
Studying real-world case studies allows entrepreneurs to understand the successes and failures of other businesses. Analyzing these cases provides valuable insights into effective decision-making and strategy implementation.

- Develop Data Analysis Skills:

In the age of big data, entrepreneurs must develop data analysis skills to make data-driven decisions. Learning techniques and tools for data analysis empowers entrepreneurs to leverage data for strategic planning, customer segmentation, and market analysis.

- Seek Expert Advice:
Continuous learning involves seeking expert advice when faced with complex decisions. Engaging with industry experts, consultants, or subject matter specialists provides entrepreneurs with valuable perspectives and guidance to make informed choices.

8. Cultivating a Growth Mindset:
Continuous learning nurtures a growth mindset, which is essential for entrepreneurial success.

- Embrace Curiosity:
Entrepreneurs should maintain a curious mindset, constantly seeking knowledge and asking questions. Curiosity fuels continuous learning and encourages exploration of new ideas and opportunities.

- Embrace Failure as a Learning Opportunity:
Adopting a growth mindset means viewing failures as valuable learning experiences. Entrepreneurs should analyze failures, identify lessons, and use them to improve their strategies and decision-making processes.

- Set Learning Goals:

Establishing learning goals encourages entrepreneurs to prioritize continuous learning. By setting specific objectives, entrepreneurs can focus their efforts, measure progress, and celebrate milestones along their learning journey.

- Foster a Learning Culture:

Entrepreneurs should foster a learning culture within their organization, encouraging employees to pursue professional development opportunities and providing resources for continuous learning. A supportive learning environment leads to motivated and engaged teams.

Conclusion:

Continuous learning is an integral part of the entrepreneurial mindset. It empowers entrepreneurs to stay ahead of the curve, adapt to changes, and seize opportunities. By embracing continuous learning, entrepreneurs can enhance their skills, expand their knowledge, foster innovation, and drive long-term success in their entrepreneurial endeavors.

Continuous learning is the minimum requirement for success in any field.

— Brian Tracy —

AZ QUOTES

Chapter 9: Building a Strong Brand

In today's competitive business landscape, building a strong brand is essential for long-term success. This chapter explores the importance of brand building for entrepreneurs and provides insights on how to create and nurture a compelling brand identity.

1. Understanding Brand Identity:

Brand identity encompasses the unique characteristics, values, and image associated with a business. Building a strong brand identity is crucial for differentiation and building customer loyalty.

- Define Your Brand Values:

Clearly articulate the core values that your brand represents. These values will serve as a guiding framework for all brand-related decisions and actions.

- Craft a Brand Mission Statement:

Develop a concise and impactful mission statement that communicates your brand's purpose and the value it aims to deliver to customers. A compelling mission statement helps establish an emotional connection with your target audience.

- Determine Your Unique Selling Proposition (USP):

Identify the unique features, benefits, or qualities that set your brand apart from competitors. Your USP should clearly communicate the value your brand offers and why customers should choose your products or services over alternatives.

2. Conducting Market Research:

Thorough market research is essential for understanding your target audience, competitors, and industry trends. This knowledge forms the foundation for effective brand building.

- Identify Target Audience:

Define your ideal customer profile by considering demographics, psychographics, and purchasing behaviors. Understanding your target audience's needs and preferences allows you to tailor your brand messaging and experiences to resonate with them.

- Analyze Competitors:

Conduct a competitive analysis to identify the strengths and weaknesses of your competitors' brands. This analysis helps you differentiate your brand and identify opportunities for improvement.

- Monitor Industry Trends:

Stay updated on industry trends, consumer behaviors, and emerging technologies. This knowledge enables you to adapt your brand strategy to meet changing market demands.

3. Developing Brand Messaging:

Clear and consistent brand messaging helps establish your brand's identity and resonate with your target audience.

- Craft a Brand Story: Develop a compelling narrative that communicates your brand's history, values, and mission. A well-crafted brand story creates an emotional connection with customers and helps differentiate your brand in a meaningful way.

- Define Brand Voice and Tone:
Determine the personality, tone, and style of communication that aligns with your brand's values and resonates with your target audience. Consistency in brand voice across all channels ensures a cohesive brand experience.

- Create a Tagline:
A memorable and impactful tagline can encapsulate your brand's essence and value proposition. A well-crafted tagline can leave a lasting impression and serve as a concise representation of your brand.

4. Designing Visual Brand Elements:
Visual brand elements create a visual identity that reflects your brand's personality and captures attention.

- Design a Logo:
Create a visually appealing and memorable logo that represents your brand's identity. Your logo should be versatile, easily recognizable, and scalable across various marketing materials.

- Choose Color Palette and Typography:

Select colors and typography that align with your brand's personality and values. Consistency in color palette and typography creates visual harmony and enhances brand recognition.

- Develop Brand Visuals:

Establish guidelines for imagery, graphics, and visual elements that represent your brand. Consistency in visual style creates a cohesive and recognizable brand identity.

5. Delivering Consistent Brand Experience:

Consistency is key to building a strong brand. Delivering a consistent brand experience across all touchpoints fosters trust, loyalty, and brand recognition.

- Brand Guidelines:

Develop brand guidelines that outline the correct usage of your brand elements, including logo, colors, typography, and tone of voice. These guidelines serve as a reference for maintaining brand consistency across all marketing and communication materials.

- Customer Experience:

Ensure that every interaction customers have with your brand reflects your brand's values and promise. From product packaging to customer service, prioritize delivering a consistent

6. Establishing Brand Positioning:

Brand positioning is the strategic placement of your brand in the minds of your target audience. It helps differentiate your brand from competitors and shapes how customers perceive your offerings.

- Identify Brand Personality:
Define the personality traits that align with your brand and resonate with your target audience. This helps create a distinct brand personality that sets you apart.

- Determine Brand Associations:
Identify the key attributes, emotions, and values you want your brand to be associated with. Consistently delivering on these associations helps build a strong brand identity.

- Communicate Unique Value Proposition:
Clearly communicate the unique value your brand offers to customers. Highlight what sets you apart and how your products or services solve their problems or fulfil their needs better than competitors.

7. Building Brand Awareness and Visibility:
To build a strong brand, entrepreneurs need to ensure their brand is visible and memorable to their target audience.

- Develop a Comprehensive Marketing Strategy:
Create a marketing plan that encompasses various channels, including digital marketing, social

media, traditional advertising, content marketing, and public relations. A well-rounded marketing strategy increases brand visibility and reach.

- Leverage Social Media Platforms:
Utilize social media platforms to engage with your audience, share valuable content, and showcase your brand's personality. Actively listen to customer feedback and respond promptly, fostering positive brand interactions.

- Influencer Partnerships:
Collaborate with influencers or industry experts who align with your brand values and have a relevant following. Their endorsement can help amplify brand visibility and reach new audiences.

8. Cultivating Brand Loyalty:
Building brand loyalty is essential for long-term success. Loyal customers not only make repeat purchases but also become brand advocates, spreading positive word-of-mouth and attracting new customers.

- Provide Exceptional Customer Experience:
Focus on delivering exceptional customer service at every touchpoint. Personalize interactions, promptly address customer concerns, and go the extra mile to exceed expectations.

- Build a community:
Foster a sense of community around your brand. Encourage customer engagement, create opportunities

for customers to connect with each other, and reward loyalty through exclusive offers or loyalty programs.

- Encourage User-Generated Content:
Encourage customers to share their experiences with your brand through reviews, testimonials, and social media posts. User-generated content adds authenticity and builds trust among potential customers.

9. Evolving and Adapting the Brand:
A strong brand is not static but evolves and adapts to changing market conditions and customer preferences.

- Monitor Brand Performance:
Continuously monitor brand performance through metrics such as brand awareness, customer satisfaction, and market share. Regularly evaluate and analyze data to identify areas for improvement.

- Conduct Brand Audits:
Periodically conduct brand audits to assess the consistency and effectiveness of your brand elements, messaging, and customer perception. Identify areas that need adjustment or enhancement.

- Embrace Brand Evolution:
As your business grows and market dynamics change, be willing to evolve your brand strategy. This

may include repositioning, refreshing visual elements, or expanding target audience segments.

Conclusion:

Building a strong brand is a fundamental aspect of entrepreneurial success. By developing a clear brand identity, conducting market research, delivering consistent brand experiences, and cultivating brand loyalty, entrepreneurs can create a compelling brand that resonates with their target audience, differentiates them from competitors, and drives long-term growth and success.

Design is the silent ambassador of your brand.

Chapter 10: Creating a Culture of Innovation

1. Understanding the Importance of Innovation:

- *Embracing a Growth Mindset:*

Encourage a growth mindset among employees, where they believe that their abilities and skills can be developed through dedication and hard work. This mindset encourages continuous learning, exploration, and the pursuit of new ideas.

- *Aligning Innovation with Business Strategy*:

Ensure that innovation efforts are closely aligned with the overall business strategy. Clearly define innovation goals and objectives that support the long-term vision and mission of the organization.

- *Building an Innovation Ecosystem:*

Create an ecosystem that fosters innovation by collaborating with external partners, such as startups, research institutions, or industry experts. This collaboration can bring fresh perspectives, access to new technologies, and opportunities for co-creation.

2. Nurturing an Environment of Psychological Safety:

- *Encouraging Open Communication:*

Foster an environment where open communication is encouraged at all levels of the organization. Create channels for employees to share their ideas, concerns, and feedback without fear of judgment or retribution.

- Promoting Trust and Respect:

Build a culture of trust and respect where everyone's contributions are valued. Encourage leaders to actively listen, show empathy, and be open to diverse perspectives, creating an environment where innovative ideas can flourish.

- Empowering Decision-Making:

Empower employees to make decisions and take ownership of their work. Provide them with autonomy and support to explore new ideas and experiment with innovative approaches.

3. Providing Resources and Support

- Allocating Time and Budget: Dedicate specific time and budget for innovation-related activities. This demonstrates a commitment to innovation and allows employees to focus on exploring new ideas without neglecting their core responsibilities.

- Offering Training and Development: Invest in training programs that equip employees with the necessary skills and knowledge to foster innovation. Provide workshops on creative problem-solving, design thinking, or other relevant methodologies.

- Creating an Innovation Incubator:

Establish a designated space or program where employees can incubate and develop innovative ideas. This can be a physical innovation lab or a virtual platform that provides resources, mentorship, and collaboration opportunities.

4. Encouraging Cross-Pollination of Ideas:

- *Cross-Functional Collaboration:*
Facilitate cross-functional collaboration by creating opportunities for employees from different departments or teams to collaborate on projects or share their expertise. This promotes the exchange of ideas, diverse perspectives, and encourages innovative thinking.

- *Networking and External Engagement:*
Encourage employees to engage in external networking events, industry conferences, or professional associations. These opportunities expose them to new ideas, emerging trends, and best practices, which can inspire innovation within the organization.

- *Innovation Champions and Ambassadors:*
Identify and empower innovation champions within the organization. These individuals can serve as ambassadors for innovation, promoting the importance of creativity, and encouraging others to embrace innovative thinking.

5. Recognizing and Rewarding Innovation:

- *Establishing Innovation Metrics:*

Define clear metrics and indicators to measure and evaluate innovation efforts. These metrics can include the number of implemented ideas, revenue generated from new products or services, or improvements in operational efficiency resulting from innovative processes.

- Implementing Recognition Programs:
Develop formal or informal recognition programs that acknowledge and celebrate employees' innovative contributions. This can include rewards, incentives, or public recognition in company-wide communications, fostering a culture that values and encourages innovation.

- Continuous Learning and Improvement:
Encourage a mindset of continuous learning and improvement. Celebrate not only successful innovations but also failed attempts that provide valuable insights and lessons. Create mechanisms for sharing and learning from both successes and failures.

Conclusion:
Creating a culture of innovation requires deliberate efforts to foster an environment that encourages creativity, risk-taking, and collaboration. By nurturing psychological safety, providing resources and support, promoting cross-pollination of ideas, and recognizing and rewarding innovation

---

Chapter 11: Managing Time and Priorities

Effective time management and prioritization are vital skills for entrepreneurs seeking to maximize productivity, achieve their goals, and maintain a healthy work-life balance. This chapter explores various strategies and techniques to help entrepreneurs manage their time and priorities efficiently, enabling them to optimize their productivity and make the most of their available resources.

A. Understanding the Importance of Time Management:

Effective time management is crucial for entrepreneurs to optimize their productivity, achieve their goals, and maintain a healthy work-life balance. Here are more detailed points on the importance of time management:

1. Resource Optimization:

Time is a limited resource that cannot be replenished. Entrepreneurs who manage their time effectively can make the most of this valuable resource. By prioritizing tasks, allocating time to important activities, and avoiding time-wasting activities, entrepreneurs can maximize their output and accomplish more within a given time frame.

2. Improved Productivity:

Effective time management techniques, such as prioritization and task scheduling, help entrepreneurs enhance their productivity. By identifying high-priority tasks and allocating focused time for their completion, entrepreneurs can avoid procrastination, minimize distractions, and stay on track to achieve their objectives.

3. Reduced Stress:

Poor time management often leads to increased stress levels. Entrepreneurs who struggle to manage their time may feel overwhelmed, rushed, or constantly behind schedule. This stress can negatively impact their performance and well-being. However, by implementing effective time management strategies, entrepreneurs can reduce stress levels, maintain a sense of control, and approach their work with a calm and focused mindset.

4. Enhanced Decision Making:

Time management allows entrepreneurs to allocate sufficient time for important decision-making processes. By organizing their time effectively, entrepreneurs can gather the necessary information, analyze options, and make well-informed decisions. This structured approach reduces the likelihood of hasty decisions based on limited information.

5. Increased Opportunities:

Effective time management enables entrepreneurs to seize opportunities as they arise. By managing their time well, entrepreneurs can be responsive and agile in capturing potential business prospects, networking, and pursuing new ventures. They are more likely to identify and capitalize on opportunities that align with their goals and strategies.

6. Improved Work-Life Balance:

Time management plays a critical role in maintaining a healthy work-life balance. Entrepreneurs who effectively manage their time can allocate dedicated periods for work, personal life, and self-care. By establishing clear boundaries and prioritizing both professional and personal commitments, entrepreneurs can enjoy a more fulfilling and balanced lifestyle.

7. Long-term Growth and Success:

Time management is a foundational skill that supports long-term growth and success. By investing time wisely in activities that align with strategic objectives, entrepreneurs can make consistent progress toward their goals. Effective time management also allows entrepreneurs to allocate time for continuous learning, skill development, and innovation, ensuring their businesses stay competitive and adaptable in a rapidly evolving market.

B. Setting Clear Goals and Priorities:

Setting clear goals and priorities is a fundamental aspect of effective time management. It provides entrepreneurs with a sense of direction and ensures that their time and energy are allocated to activities that align with their vision and objectives. Here are more detailed points on the importance of setting clear goals and priorities:

1. Goal Clarity:

Clear goals provide entrepreneurs with a specific target to work towards. By defining goals that are specific, measurable, attainable, relevant, and time-bound (SMART), entrepreneurs can create a roadmap for success. Clarity about what needs to be accomplished allows entrepreneurs to prioritize tasks and allocate their time and resources effectively.

2. Alignment with Vision and Strategy:

Setting clear goals and priorities ensures that they are aligned with the overall vision and strategy of the business. Entrepreneurs can identify goals that contribute directly to the long-term success and growth of their venture. This alignment provides focus and direction, allowing entrepreneurs to make decisions and allocate resources based on strategic objectives.

3. Differentiating Importance and Urgency:

Not all tasks or activities have equal importance or urgency. Entrepreneurs need to distinguish between tasks that are important and those that are urgent. Important tasks align with long-term goals, while urgent tasks require immediate attention. By understanding the difference, entrepreneurs can prioritize their time and effort on activities that have the most significant impact on their business objectives.

4. Prioritization Techniques:

Various prioritization techniques can help entrepreneurs manage their time effectively. Some common techniques include:

- *Eisenhower Matrix:*

This framework categorizes tasks into four quadrants based on their importance and urgency. It helps entrepreneurs prioritize tasks by identifying what needs to be done now, what can be scheduled, what can be delegated, and what can be eliminated.

- *ABC Analysis:*

This technique involves assigning priorities to tasks by labelling them as A (high priority), B (medium priority), or C (low priority) based on their impact and deadline. It helps entrepreneurs focus on high-priority tasks first while ensuring that other tasks are not neglected.

- *Pareto Principle:*

Also known as the 80/20 rule, this principle states that approximately 80% of outcomes result from 20% of inputs. Entrepreneurs can apply this principle by identifying the key tasks or activities that generate the most significant impact and prioritizing them accordingly.

5. Focus on High-Value Tasks:

Setting clear goals and priorities enables entrepreneurs to focus their time and energy on high-value tasks that contribute directly to their objectives. By identifying tasks that align with their core competencies and have the most significant impact on their business, entrepreneurs can allocate their resources wisely and avoid getting caught up in low-value, time-consuming activities.

6. Flexibility and Adaptability:

While clear goals and priorities provide a framework, entrepreneurs must also be flexible and adaptable. The business landscape is dynamic, and unforeseen circumstances may require adjustments to goals and priorities. Entrepreneurs should regularly evaluate and reassess their goals, making necessary modifications to align with changing market conditions or new opportunities.

Setting clear goals and priorities is essential for entrepreneurs to stay focused, make informed decisions, and manage their time effectively. By aligning goals with their vision, differentiating importance and urgency, utilizing prioritization techniques, and focusing on high-value tasks, entrepreneurs can enhance their productivity, achieve their objectives, and drive the success of their venture.

C. Effective Time Management Strategies:

Implementing effective time management strategies is crucial for entrepreneurs to optimize their productivity, make efficient use of their time, and achieve their goals. Here are more detailed points on effective time management strategies:

1. Time Blocking:

Time blocking involves allocating specific blocks of time for different tasks or activities. By creating a schedule and dedicating focused time to particular tasks, entrepreneurs can enhance their concentration and productivity. This strategy helps prevent distractions and ensures that essential tasks receive the attention they deserve.

2. Prioritization and Task Management:

Prioritizing tasks is a fundamental aspect of effective time management. Entrepreneurs should assess their to-do lists or task backlog and identify tasks based on their urgency and importance. They can then allocate their time and effort accordingly, focusing on high-priority tasks that align with their goals and have a significant impact on their business.

3. The 80/20 Rule:

The Pareto Principle, also known as the 80/20 rule, states that 80% of results come from 20% of efforts. Entrepreneurs can apply this principle by identifying the tasks or activities that generate the most significant results and prioritizing them. By focusing on the critical few tasks that yield the highest impact, entrepreneurs can optimize their time and productivity.

4. Time Audit:

Conducting a time audit involves tracking how time is spent on various activities throughout the day. This assessment helps entrepreneurs identify time-wasting activities, unproductive habits, or areas where time could be better utilized. By gaining awareness of how time is allocated, entrepreneurs can make necessary adjustments to improve efficiency.

5. Avoiding Multitasking:

While multitasking may seem efficient, it often leads to decreased productivity and increased errors. Instead of trying to juggle multiple tasks simultaneously, entrepreneurs should focus on one task at a time. By giving full attention to each task, entrepreneurs can complete them more effectively and efficiently.

6. Delegation and Outsourcing:

Entrepreneurs should recognize that they cannot do everything themselves. Delegating tasks to team members or outsourcing non-essential activities can free up time for higher-value tasks. Entrepreneurs should identify tasks that can be effectively handled by others and trust their team to take on responsibilities, enabling them to focus on strategic and growth-oriented activities.

7. Automation and Technology:

Utilizing technology and automation tools can streamline processes and save time. Entrepreneurs should explore software, apps, and tools that can automate repetitive tasks, improve organization, and enhance efficiency. From project management tools to email automation systems, leveraging technology can help entrepreneurs optimize their time and maximize productivity.

8. Time for Breaks and Rest:

While it may seem counterintuitive, taking regular breaks and allowing for rest is essential for maintaining productivity and avoiding burnout. Breaks help rejuvenate the mind, improve focus, and enhance overall well-being. Entrepreneurs should schedule short breaks throughout the day and allocate time for self-care activities to recharge and maintain optimal performance.

9. Saying No and Setting Boundaries:

Entrepreneurs often face numerous requests, meetings, and obligations. Learning to say no and setting clear boundaries is vital for effective time management. Entrepreneurs should evaluate each request or commitment and assess its alignment with their goals and priorities. By selectively accepting commitments, entrepreneurs can avoid overloading their schedules and focus on high-value activities.

10. Continuous Improvement:

Effective time management is an ongoing process that requires continuous evaluation and improvement.

Entrepreneurs should regularly review their time management strategies, assess their effectiveness, and make necessary adjustments. Experimenting with different techniques, seeking feedback, and learning from experiences can help entrepreneurs refine their approach to time management.

D. Managing Distractions and Enhancing Focus:

In today's fast-paced and digitally connected world, managing distractions and enhancing focus is essential for entrepreneurs to maintain productivity and achieve their goals. Here are more detailed points on managing distractions and enhancing focus:

1. Identify Common Distractions:

Start by identifying the common distractions that hinder your focus. These may include social media notifications, email alerts, noisy environments, or interruptions from colleagues. By understanding the specific distractions that impact you the most, you can develop strategies to minimize their impact.

2. Create a Distraction-Free Environment:

Designate a workspace that is free from distractions. This could be a dedicated office, a quiet corner in a café, or a co-working space. Remove or minimize potential distractions such as excessive clutter, unrelated materials, or personal items that can divert your attention.

3. Establish Clear Boundaries:

Communicate with others, whether it's your team, family members, or friends, about your need for uninterrupted focus. Set clear boundaries and establish specific periods of uninterrupted work time during which you can avoid interruptions and stay focused on your tasks.

4. Practice Time Blocking:

Allocate specific time blocks for focused work and avoid multitasking during these periods. During these blocks, eliminate or minimize distractions by turning off notifications, closing unnecessary tabs or apps, and setting your phone to silent mode. By dedicating uninterrupted time to important tasks, you can maintain concentration and complete them efficiently.

5. Utilize Productivity Tools:

Leverage productivity tools and apps that can help manage distractions. These tools can block specific websites or apps during designated work periods, track time spent on different tasks, or provide ambient background noise to enhance concentration. Find tools that align with your preferences and needs to optimize your focus and minimize distractions.

6. Practice Mindfulness and Meditation:

Incorporate mindfulness and meditation practices into your routine to enhance focus and reduce mental clutter. Taking a few minutes each day to engage in mindful breathing exercises or meditation can help clear your mind, increase self-awareness, and improve your ability to concentrate on tasks.

7. Break Tasks into Manageable Chunks:

Large or complex tasks can be overwhelming and easily lead to loss of focus. Break these tasks into smaller, more manageable chunks. By focusing on one small part at a time, you can maintain a sense of progress and accomplishment, which can boost motivation and concentration.

8. Establish a Routine:

Establishing a consistent routine can help train your mind to focus during specific times. By creating a habit of working on specific tasks during designated periods, your brain becomes accustomed to the focused work mode, making it easier to stay on track and avoid distractions.

9. Practice the Pomodoro Technique:

The Pomodoro Technique involves working in focused sprints of 25 minutes, followed by a short break of 5 minutes. After completing four cycles, take a longer break of 15-30 minutes. This structured approach to work and breaks can help maintain focus, combat fatigue, and enhance productivity.

10. Take Care of Physical and Mental Well-being:

Physical and mental well-being play a significant role in enhancing focus. Prioritize regular exercise, healthy eating, and sufficient sleep to ensure your body and mind are in optimal condition. Additionally, manage stress levels through relaxation techniques, such as deep breathing exercises or engaging in hobbies that bring joy and relaxation.

11. Set Clear Goals and Priorities:

Having clear goals and priorities provides direction and focus. When you are clear about what needs to be accomplished, it becomes easier to stay focused and avoid getting side-tracked by unrelated tasks or distractions. Regularly review and prioritize your tasks to ensure you are investing your time in activities that align with your goals.

E. Work-Life Balance and Self-Care:

Maintaining a healthy work-life balance and prioritizing self-care are essential for the well-being and long-term success of entrepreneurs. Here are more detailed points on work-life balance and self-care:

1. Define Your Priorities:

Clearly identify your personal and professional priorities. Determine what truly matters to you in both areas of your life. This will help you establish boundaries and make conscious decisions about how you allocate your time and energy.

2. Set Realistic Expectations:

Recognize that achieving a perfect balance between work and personal life is challenging. Instead, focus on setting realistic expectations for yourself. Understand that there will be times when work requires more attention, but also ensure you create space for personal and family commitments.

3. Establish Boundaries:

Set clear boundaries between work and personal life. Determine specific times for work and leisure activities, and stick to them as much as possible. Communicate these boundaries to your team, colleagues, and loved ones, so they understand your availability and can respect your personal time.

4. Delegate and Outsource:

Learn to delegate tasks that don't necessarily require your direct involvement. By assigning responsibilities to capable team members or outsourcing certain activities, you can free up time for other important aspects of your life.

5. Practice Time Blocking:

Allocate specific time blocks for work, family, hobbies, and self-care activities. This ensures that all aspects of your life receive dedicated attention and prevents one area from overpowering the others.

6. Unplug and Disconnect:

Schedule regular periods of unplugging from work-related activities, such as emails and calls. Create boundaries around technology use during personal time to allow for relaxation, quality time with loved ones, and pursuing hobbies and interests.

7. Prioritize Self-Care:

Make self-care a non-negotiable part of your routine. Prioritize activities that nourish your physical, mental, and emotional well-being. This can include exercise, meditation, reading, spending time in nature, practicing mindfulness, or engaging in hobbies that bring you joy.

8. Learn to Say No:

Understand your limitations and learn to say no to commitments that don't align with your priorities or may overwhelm your schedule. Saying no allows you to protect your time and focus on activities that truly matter to you.

9. Foster Supportive Relationships:

Surround yourself with a strong support system of family, friends, and colleagues who understand the challenges you face as an entrepreneur. Seek their support, advice, and encouragement when needed, and reciprocate by being supportive of their endeavors as well.

10. Practice Mindfulness:

Incorporate mindfulness practices into your daily routine to stay present and reduce stress. Mindfulness exercises, such as deep breathing, meditation, or journaling, can help you cultivate a sense of calm and balance amidst the demands of entrepreneurship.

11. Schedule Regular Breaks and Vacations:

Plan regular breaks and vacations to recharge and rejuvenate. Taking time away from work allows you to disconnect, gain perspective, and return with renewed energy and creativity.

12. Reflect and Evaluate:

Regularly reflect on your work-life balance and self-care practices. Evaluate whether you are honoring your boundaries, making time for self-care, and maintaining a sense of fulfillment in all areas of your life. Make adjustments as needed to ensure you are living a balanced and fulfilling entrepreneurial journey.

Remember, work-life balance and self-care are ongoing practices that require conscious effort and adaptation. By prioritizing your well-being and nurturing a healthy balance between work and personal life, you can sustain your entrepreneurial journey and thrive in all aspects of your life.

"Creativity is thinking up new things. Innovation is doing new things."

Theodore Levitt

<u>Chapter 12: Building and Managing High-Performing Teams</u>

Building and managing high-performing teams is a critical skill for entrepreneurs. A cohesive and effective team can drive innovation, productivity, and overall success. In this chapter, we will explore in detail the key principles and strategies for building and managing high-performing teams:

1. Defining Team Roles and Responsibilities:

Clearly define the roles and responsibilities of each team member. Ensure that the roles are aligned with their strengths, skills, and expertise. This promotes clarity, reduces conflicts, and enables each team member to contribute their best.

2. Hiring the Right Talent:

Building a high-performing team starts with hiring the right people. Look for individuals who not only possess the required skills and experience but also align with the company's values and culture. Seek diverse perspectives and backgrounds that can contribute to a well-rounded team.

3. Fostering Trust and Psychological Safety:

Create an environment of trust and psychological safety within the team. Encourage open communication, active listening, and respect for different ideas and opinions. When team members feel safe to share their thoughts and take risks, it fosters collaboration, creativity, and innovation.

4. Setting Clear Goals and Expectations:

Establish clear goals, objectives, and expectations for the team. Communicate these effectively and ensure that everyone understands their individual and collective responsibilities. Clear goals provide a sense of direction, alignment, and motivation for the team to work towards shared objectives.

5. Promoting Effective Communication:

Encourage open and transparent communication among team members. Foster an environment where ideas and feedback can be freely expressed. Utilize various communication channels, such as team meetings, project management tools, and collaboration platforms, to ensure effective information sharing and collaboration.

6. Building a Collaborative Culture:

Cultivate a culture of collaboration, where teamwork is valued and encouraged. Promote cross-functional collaboration, encourage knowledge sharing, and facilitate opportunities for team members to collaborate on projects or solve problems together. This creates synergy and maximizes the collective capabilities of the team.

7. Providing Growth and Development Opportunities:

Support the growth and development of team members by providing training, mentoring, and coaching opportunities. Invest in their professional development to enhance their skills and expertise. When team members feel supported and empowered to grow, they are more engaged and motivated to contribute to the team's success.

8. Encouraging Innovation and Creativity:

Foster an environment that values and rewards innovation and creativity. Encourage team members to think outside the box, explore new ideas, and challenge the status quo. Create avenues for brainstorming, idea generation, and experimentation, allowing the team to explore innovative solutions and approaches.

9. Resolving Conflict Constructively:

Conflict is inevitable within any team. However, it is essential to address conflicts promptly and constructively. Encourage open dialogue, active listening, and mutual respect when resolving conflicts. Provide a safe space for team members to express their concerns and work towards mutually agreeable solutions.

10. Recognizing and Celebrating Achievements:

Acknowledge and celebrate individual and team achievements. Regularly recognize and appreciate the efforts and contributions of team members. This boosts morale, fosters a positive team culture, and reinforces a sense of accomplishment and motivation.

11. Empowering Decision Making:

Empower team members to make decisions and take ownership of their work. Delegate authority and responsibility appropriately, allowing team members to contribute their ideas and take initiative. When individuals feel empowered, they become more engaged and committed to the team's success.

12. Managing Performance and Providing Feedback:

Regularly assess and manage the performance of team members. Provide timely and constructive feedback to help them improve and grow. Establish performance metrics and goals, and provide ongoing support and coaching to ensure continuous improvement.

"When a team outgrows individual performance and learns team confidence, excellence becomes a reality."

- Joe Paterno

Chapter 13: Scaling and Growing Your Business

Scaling and growing a business is a pivotal stage for entrepreneurs. It involves expanding operations, increasing market share, and maximizing profitability. This chapter delves deeper into the strategies and considerations required to effectively scale and grow your business.

Section 1: Assessing Market Potential and Opportunities

1. Conducting Market Research:
- Identify target markets, customer segments, and emerging trends.
- Analyze customer needs, preferences, and pain points.
- Evaluate the competitive landscape and identify gaps or untapped opportunities.

2. Identifying Growth Opportunities:
- Assess the potential for product diversification, geographic expansion, or entering new markets.
- Identify strategic partnerships or collaborations that can accelerate growth.
- Evaluate the scalability of your business model and its ability to meet increasing demand.

Section 2: Strategic Planning and Goal Setting

1. Developing a Growth Strategy:
- Define your vision, mission, and long-term goals.
- Formulate a growth strategy aligned with your core values and capabilities.
- Break down objectives into actionable steps and timelines.

2. SWOT Analysis:

- Evaluate strengths, weaknesses, opportunities, and threats.
- Capitalize on strengths and opportunities while addressing weaknesses and mitigating threats.
- Identify areas for improvement and develop strategies to overcome challenges.

Section 3: Operational Efficiency and Systems

1. Streamlining Processes:
- Identify and eliminate bottlenecks in your operational workflows.
- Automate repetitive tasks to improve efficiency and productivity.
- Implement quality control measures to ensure consistency and customer satisfaction.

2. Scalable Infrastructure:
- Assess your infrastructure's capacity to support growth.
- Invest in technology, equipment, and facilities as needed.
- Consider cloud-based solutions for scalability and cost-effectiveness.

Section 4: Talent Acquisition and Development

1. Building a High-Performing Team:
- Define roles and responsibilities to support business growth.

- Recruit individuals with the right skills, experience, and cultural fit.
- Foster a positive work environment that promotes collaboration and innovation.

2. Continuous Learning and Development:
- Provide training and development opportunities to enhance employees' skills.
- Encourage knowledge sharing and cross-functional collaboration.
- Invest in leadership development to empower managers and future leaders.

Section 5: Financial Planning and Funding

1. Financial Forecasting:
- Develop realistic financial projections based on growth objectives.
- Monitor key financial metrics and adjust strategies accordingly.
- Identify potential funding gaps and implement contingency plans.

2. Funding Options:
- Explore different funding sources, such as loans, investments, or grants.
- Present a compelling business case to attract investors or secure financing.
- Consider bootstrapping and revenue reinvestment to maintain control and sustainability.

<u>Section 6:</u> Market Expansion and Customer Acquisition

1. Marketing and Sales Strategy:
- Define your target audience and develop a tailored marketing strategy.
- Leverage digital marketing channels to reach and engage a broader customer base.
- Establish strategic partnerships to access new markets or distribution channels.

2. Customer Relationship Management:
- Nurture existing customer relationships and encourage repeat business.
- Implement customer feedback mechanisms to improve products and services.
- Personalize customer experiences to build loyalty and advocacy.

<u>Section 7:</u> Managing Risks and Challenges

1. Risk Assessment and Mitigation:
- Identify potential risks associated with growth plans.
- Develop risk management strategies to minimize the impact of unforeseen events.
- Regularly review and update risk mitigation plans as the business evolves.

2. Agility and Adaptability:

- Embrace a culture of agility and adaptability to respond to market changes.
- Continuously monitor industry trends, competitor activities, and customer demands.

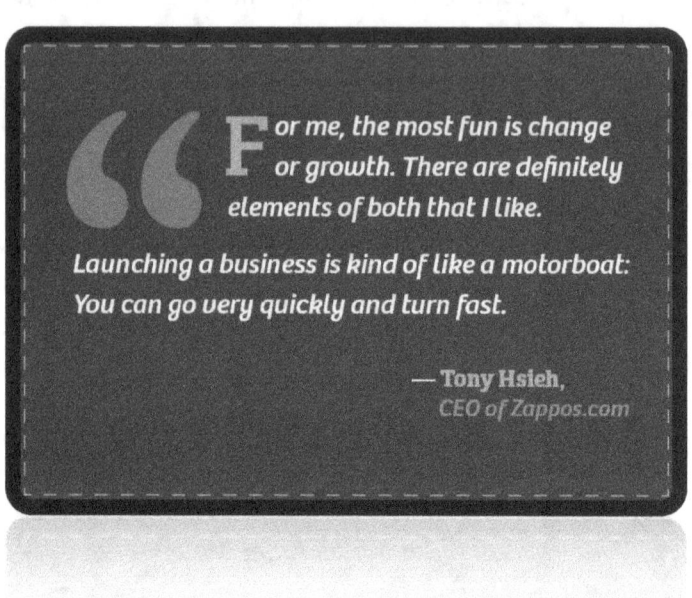

For me, the most fun is change or growth. There are definitely elements of both that I like.

Launching a business is kind of like a motorboat: You can go very quickly and turn fast.

— Tony Hsieh,
CEO of Zappos.com

Chapter 14: Navigating Legal and Regulatory Issues

As an entrepreneur, navigating the complex landscape of legal and regulatory requirements is essential for the success and sustainability of your business. This chapter explores the key considerations and strategies for effectively managing legal and regulatory issues.

Section 1: Understanding Legal Structures

1. Choosing the Right Legal Structure:

- Evaluate different legal structures such as sole proprietorship, partnership, limited liability company (LLC), or corporation.
- Consider factors such as liability protection, taxation, ownership, and management flexibility.
- Consult with legal professionals or business advisors to determine the most suitable structure for your business.

2. Registering Your Business:

- Understand the process and requirements for business registration in your jurisdiction.
- Obtain necessary permits, licenses, and registrations applicable to your industry and location.
- Comply with local, state, and federal regulations governing business operations.

Section 2: Contracts and Agreements

1. Contract Management:

- Develop a clear understanding of contract law and its application to your business.
- Draft and negotiate contracts that protect your interests and clearly define rights and obligations.
- Regularly review and update contracts to ensure they align with changing business needs.

2. Intellectual Property Protection:

- Identify and protect your intellectual property assets, including trademarks, copyrights, and patents.
- Conduct a thorough search to ensure your intellectual property does not infringe on others' rights.
- Consider consulting with intellectual property attorneys to navigate the complexities of IP protection.

Section 3: Employment Laws and Regulations

1. Hiring and Employee Management:
- Understand and comply with employment laws related to hiring, wages, working hours, and benefits.
- Develop clear employment contracts and policies that align with local labour regulations.
- Implement fair employment practices to promote a positive work environment and prevent discrimination.

2. Protecting Confidentiality and Trade Secrets:
- Implement confidentiality agreements and non-disclosure agreements (NDAs) to protect sensitive business information.
- Safeguard trade secrets and proprietary information through proper documentation and security measures.
- Educate employees about the importance of confidentiality and their legal obligations.

Section 4: Financial and Tax Compliance

1. Financial Recordkeeping:
- Maintain accurate financial records in compliance with accounting standards and regulations.

- Implement proper bookkeeping practices and recordkeeping systems.

- Prepare financial statements and reports as required by law and for tax purposes.

2. Tax Compliance:

- Understand the tax obligations specific to your business structure and industry.

- Stay updated on tax laws, regulations, and filing deadlines.

- Consider consulting with tax professionals to ensure accurate and timely tax filings.

Section 5: Consumer Protection and Privacy

1. Consumer Protection Laws:

- Comply with consumer protection laws governing advertising, product labelling, warranties, and refunds.

- Maintain transparency and honesty in your business practices to protect consumer rights.

- Establish effective customer service and complaint resolution processes.

2. Data Privacy and Security:

- Understand data protection laws and regulations related to the collection, storage, and use of customer data.

- Implement robust data security measures to safeguard sensitive customer information.

- Develop a privacy policy that clearly communicates how customer data is handled and protected.

<u>Section 6:</u> Compliance and Risk Management

1. Regulatory Compliance:
- Stay informed about industry-specific regulations and comply with applicable laws.
- Regularly assess your business practices and operations to ensure ongoing compliance.
- Establish internal controls and procedures to mitigate compliance risks.

2. Legal Dispute Resolution:
- Develop a plan for handling legal disputes, including alternative dispute resolution methods such as mediation or arbitration.
- Maintain open communication with legal advisors and seek professional guidance when facing legal challenges.

<u>Chapter 15: Giving Back and Making a Positive Impact</u>

In today's world, businesses are not just seen as profit-making entities but also as agents of change and contributors to the greater good. Chapter 17 explores the importance of giving back and making a positive impact through corporate social responsibility (CSR) initiatives. This chapter delves deeper into the strategies and practical steps entrepreneurs can take to integrate social responsibility into their business practices.

Section 1: Understanding Corporate Social Responsibility

1. Defining Corporate Social Responsibility (CSR):
- Gain a comprehensive understanding of CSR and its significance in the business landscape.
- Recognize the ethical, social, and environmental responsibilities of businesses.
- Understand the triple bottom line approach, which encompasses people, planet, and profit.

2. Identifying Social and Environmental Issues:
- Conduct a thorough analysis of social and environmental issues relevant to your industry and local community.
- Identify areas where your business can make a meaningful impact and contribute to positive change.
- Engage stakeholders, including employees, customers, and community members, to gain insights and perspectives on priority areas.

Section 2: Developing a CSR Strategy

1. Establishing Core Values and Mission:
- Define your company's core values and how they align with social and environmental causes.
- Develop a mission statement that reflects your commitment to making a positive impact.
- Ensure that your CSR efforts are integrated into your overall business strategy and culture.

2. Setting Goals and Objectives:

- Set specific, measurable, achievable, relevant, and time-bound (SMART) goals for your CSR initiatives.
- Align your goals with your company's values and mission.
- Prioritize areas where your business can have the most significant impact.

Section 3: Implementing CSR Initiatives

1. Employee Engagement:

- Foster a culture of social responsibility within your organization.
- Encourage employees to participate in volunteer activities and community service.
- Provide paid time off for employees to engage in philanthropic endeavors.

2. Ethical Business Practices:

- Adhere to ethical business practices that promote fairness, transparency, and integrity.
- Embrace responsible sourcing and sustainable procurement practices.
- Ensure that your business operations align with ethical standards and industry best practices.

Section 4: Partnerships and Collaboration

1. Engaging with Non-profit Organizations:

- Identify non-profit organizations that align with your company's values and goals.

- Establish partnerships to support their initiatives and amplify your impact.
- Collaborate on projects and programs that address shared social or environmental challenges.

2. Collaboration with Stakeholders:
- Engage with customers, suppliers, and local communities to understand their needs and concerns.
- Collaborate on initiatives that address shared social or environmental challenges.
- Foster long-term relationships based on trust, mutual respect, and shared values.

Section 5: Measuring and Communicating Impact

1. Impact Measurement:
- Develop a robust framework for measuring the social and environmental impact of your CSR initiatives.
- Use key performance indicators (KPIs) to track progress and evaluate the effectiveness of your programs.
- Collect data and conduct regular assessments to inform decision-making and improve your initiatives.

2. Communicating Your CSR Efforts:
- Develop a comprehensive communication strategy to share your CSR initiatives with stakeholders.
- Highlight the positive impact your business is making and the progress you have achieved.
- Utilize various channels, such as social media, press releases, annual reports, and dedicated CSR sections

on your website, to effectively communicate your CSR efforts.

Conclusion:

Incorporating social responsibility into your business not only benefits society but also strengthens your brand, builds customer loyalty, and attracts socially conscious employees. By giving back and making a positive impact, entrepreneurs can contribute to a more sustainable and equitable future.

Chapter 16: Continuing the Entrepreneurial Journey

The entrepreneurial journey is an ongoing process filled with challenges, growth, and opportunities. Chapter 18 explores the importance of continuing the entrepreneurial journey beyond the initial stages of starting a business. It focuses on strategies and mindset shifts to sustain success, adapt to changes, and embrace lifelong learning.

Section 1: Embracing Growth and Adaptation

1. Embracing a Growth Mindset:

- Develop a growth mindset that sees challenges as opportunities for learning and improvement.
- Embrace a willingness to adapt, experiment, and take calculated risks.
- Cultivate a mindset that seeks continuous growth and development, both personally and professionally.

2. Navigating Change and Uncertainty:

- Recognize that change is inevitable and embrace it as an opportunity for growth.
- Develop resilience to navigate through uncertain times and adapt your business strategies accordingly.
- Stay informed about market trends, emerging technologies, and shifts in consumer behaviour to proactively respond to change.

Section 2: Fostering Innovation and Creativity

1. Encouraging a Culture of Innovation:

- Foster a culture that encourages creativity, innovation, and out-of-the-box thinking.
- Create an environment where employees feel empowered to contribute ideas and solutions.
- Establish processes for idea generation, evaluation, and implementation.

2. Embracing Technology and Digital Transformation:

- Stay updated on technological advancements relevant to your industry.

- Embrace digital transformation to streamline processes, enhance efficiency, and improve customer experience.
- Explore innovative technologies and tools that can give your business a competitive edge.

Section 3: Building Strategic Partnerships

1. Collaboration and Strategic Alliances:
- Identify potential strategic partners or alliances that can complement your business.
- Form partnerships that leverage each other's strengths and create mutual benefits.
- Collaborate with other entrepreneurs, industry experts, and organizations to share knowledge and resources.

2. Mentorship and Networking:
- Seek mentorship from experienced entrepreneurs or industry professionals who can provide guidance and insights.
- Attend industry events, conferences, and networking opportunities to expand your professional network.
- Engage in peer-to-peer learning and collaboration with other entrepreneurs.

Section 4: Balancing Work and Well-being

1. Prioritizing Self-care:
- Recognize the importance of self-care for maintaining physical, mental, and emotional well-being.

- Establish routines that include exercise, proper nutrition, and adequate rest.
- Practice mindfulness techniques and stress management strategies to maintain a healthy work-life balance.

2. Delegating and Building a Support System:
- Delegate tasks and responsibilities to capable team members to avoid burnout and focus on high-impact activities.
- Build a support system of mentors, advisors, and trusted colleagues who can provide guidance and support.
- Seek feedback and advice from your support system to gain different perspectives and insights.

Conclusion:
Continuing the entrepreneurial journey requires a commitment to personal growth, adaptability, and innovation. By embracing change, fostering a culture of innovation, building strategic partnerships, and prioritizing well-being, entrepreneurs can sustain success, overcome challenges, and thrive in an ever-evolving business landscape. Remember that the entrepreneurial journey is a lifelong pursuit of growth and learning, and each stage presents new opportunities for development and achievement.

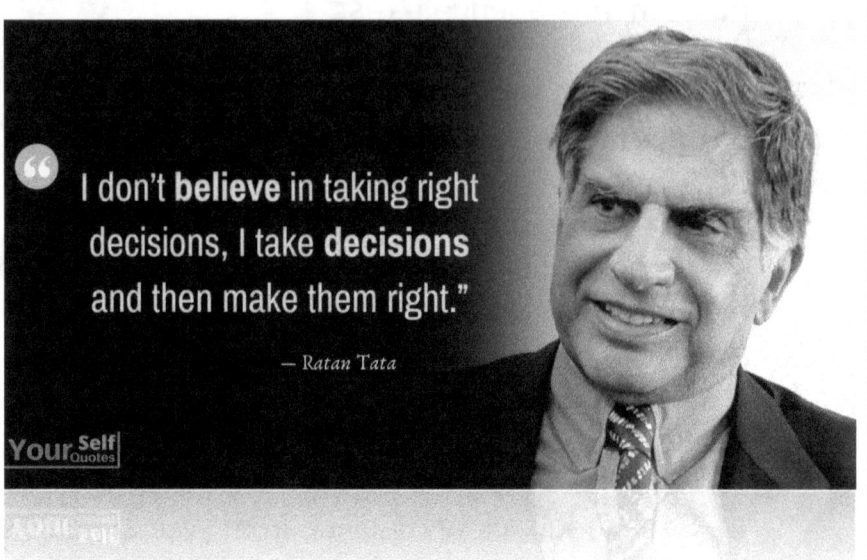

I don't **believe** in taking right decisions, I take **decisions** and then make them right."

— *Ratan Tata*

Your Self Quotes

Chapter 17: Conclusion and Call to Action

In this final chapter, we reflect on the key insights and lessons learned throughout the book and provide a compelling call to action for entrepreneurs. It serves as a reminder of the importance of the entrepreneurial mindset and encourages readers to take action and apply the knowledge gained to their own entrepreneurial endeavors.

Section 1: Reflecting on the Entrepreneurial Journey

1. Recap of Key Concepts:
- Summarize the main concepts covered in the book, highlighting the core characteristics of the entrepreneurial mindset.
- Remind readers of the challenges, strategies, and skills discussed in earlier chapters.
- Reinforce the idea that entrepreneurship is a continuous journey of growth, learning, and adaptation.

2. Lessons from Successful Entrepreneurs:
- Share inspiring stories of successful entrepreneurs who embody the entrepreneurial mindset.
- Discuss the challenges they faced, how they overcame them, and the strategies they employed.
- Extract valuable lessons from their experiences to motivate readers and provide practical insights.

Section 2: The Call to Action

1. Embracing the Entrepreneurial Mindset:
- Encourage readers to adopt and nurture the entrepreneurial mindset in their own lives and businesses.
- Highlight the benefits of cultivating traits such as resilience, creativity, adaptability, and risk-taking.
- Stress the importance of maintaining a growth mindset and continuously seeking personal and professional development.

2. Taking Action:

- Inspire readers to take action and apply the knowledge gained from the book to their entrepreneurial endeavors.

- Encourage them to set clear goals, develop action plans, and implement strategies discussed throughout the chapters.

- Emphasize the value of persistence, discipline, and accountability in turning ideas into reality.

3. Leveraging Networks and Resources:
- Encourage readers to build strong networks and seek support from mentors, peers, and industry experts.

- Highlight the importance of leveraging available resources, such as incubators, accelerators, and entrepreneurial communities.

- Emphasize the power of collaboration and strategic partnerships in driving business growth and success.

4. Making a Positive Impact:
- Inspire readers to consider the broader impact of their entrepreneurial endeavors beyond financial success.

- Encourage them to incorporate corporate social responsibility initiatives and contribute to social and environmental causes.

- Highlight the potential for businesses to be a force for positive change and encourage readers to make a difference in their communities.

Conclusion:

In conclusion, The Entrepreneurial Mindset is a comprehensive guide that explores the essential characteristics, skills, and strategies needed to thrive in the entrepreneurial world. It serves as a reminder that entrepreneurship is not just about starting a business but embarking on a lifelong journey of growth, innovation, and impact. By embracing the entrepreneurial mindset and taking action, readers can unlock their full potential, overcome challenges, and create successful and fulfilling entrepreneurial ventures. The time for action is now, so go forth and unleash your entrepreneurial spirit!